THE NATURE KIDS GUIDE TO
ROAD RUNNERS

DAVID ANDERSON

LP Media Inc. Publishing
Text copyright © 2026 by LP Media Inc.
All rights reserved.

For information address LP Media Inc. Publishing,
30012 Variolite St NW, Princeton MN 55371
www.lpmedia.org

Publication Data

Road Runners
The Nature Kid's Guide to Road Runners — First edition.

Summary: "Learn all about Road Runners, the Nature Kid Way"
— Provided by publisher.

ISBN: 979-8-89818-143-7

[1. Road Runners – Non-Fiction] I. Title.

Title: The Nature Kid's Guide to Road Runners

CONTENTS

Desert Dwellers 4

Range Roamers 6

Size Check 8

Built to Bolt 10

Sharp Senses 12

Clever Camo 14

Snack Attack 16

Speedy Strikes 18

Watch Out 20

Run Run Run 22

Zippy Zoomers 24

Day Dash 26

Solo Stars 28

Love Calls 30

Cute Chicks 32

Team Teach 34

Tough Birds 36

Spot One 38

DESERT DWELLERS

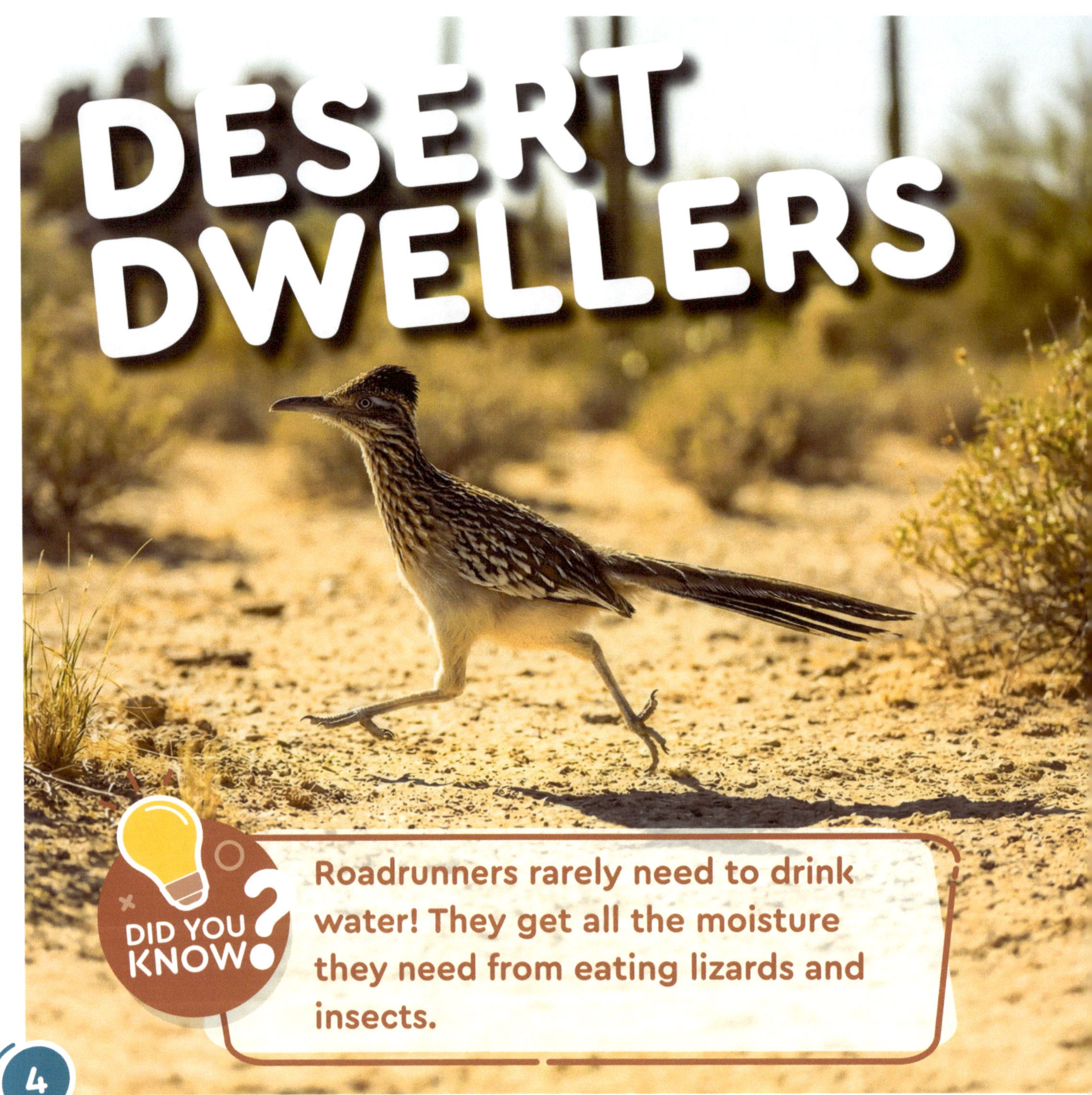

Zoom! A roadrunner races across the hot sand. Its long legs move in a blur.

Roadrunners live in hot, dry deserts. They make their homes in rocky places where rain hardly falls. These tough birds have adapted to survive where few other animals can.

Roadrunners love the heat. They live where cactus plants grow tall and scrubby bushes dot the dusty, brown land. Open ground is important so they can sprint after prey.

Roadrunners build nests in low bushes or cactus plants. The sharp spines help keep eggs safe. They also nest in small trees when they can find them.

RANGE ROAMERS

Screech! A roadrunner calls from a rocky hill. It looks for food.

Roadrunners live in the southwestern United States. They live in Mexico too. You can find them from California to Louisiana.

These birds stay in one place all year. They do not fly south for winter. Where they live is already warm, even during the winter!

Roadrunners can live in low deserts near sea level. They can also live 9,000 feet high in the mountains.

Roadrunners like to run more than fly. They can run more than 20 miles per hour!

SIZE
CHECK

Snap! A roadrunner stands tall. It stretches its long neck.

Roadrunners are about 20 to 24 inches long. That is about the length of two rulers! But they weigh only 8 to 15 ounces.

These birds have long tails. The tail makes up half their body length, and it helps them balance when they run fast.

Roadrunners stand about 10 to 12 inches tall. They are larger than robins and about as tall as a crow.

A roadrunner's wingspan is about 19 inches wide. That is wider than a basketball!

BUILT TO BOLT

Roadrunners have blue and orange skin patches behind each eye. They can flash these!

Click! A roadrunner snaps its beak shut. Its body is built for speed.

Roadrunners have bodies **adapted** for the desert. Their legs are long and strong. Each foot has four toes, with two pointing forward and two pointing backward.

Their beaks are long and curved, sometimes over 2 inches! This shape helps them grab lizards and snakes.

Roadrunners have streaky brown and white feathers. A **crest** of feathers sits on top of their head. They can raise or lower this crest to show their mood.

SHARP SENSES

Swoosh! A roadrunner spots a lizard far away. Its eyes lock on.

Roadrunners have excellent eyesight. They can see tiny prey from far away.

Their eyes sit on the sides of their head. This gives them a wide view of the desert. They can spot danger from many directions at once.

Roadrunners also have good hearing. They listen for insects and small animals moving in the brush.

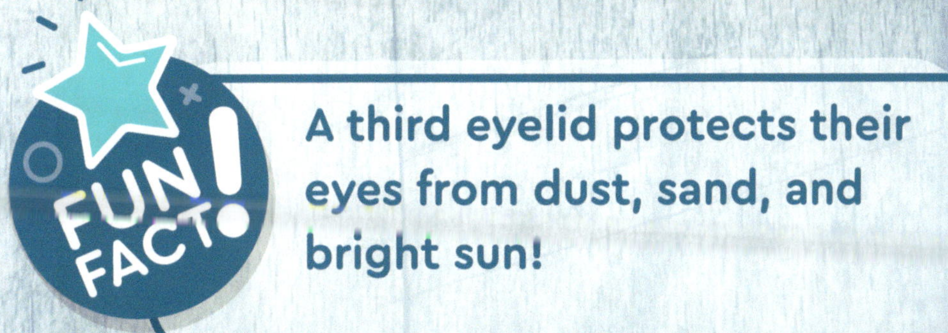

CLEVER CAMO

Baby roadrunners have dark skin. The dark skin soaks up heat. This keeps them warm at night!

Rustle! A roadrunner crouches low. It hides in the dry brush.

Roadrunners have brown, tan, and white feathers. The feathers have streaks. These colors match the desert floor. This makes it hard for **predators** to see them.

Sometimes roadrunners cannot run away. They crouch down and stay very still. Their feathers look like rocks and twigs.

Roadrunners can also hide in bushes. They slip into thick shrubs. They wait quietly. They stay until the danger passes.

SNACK ATTACK
16

Crunch! A roadrunner catches a grasshopper. Time to eat!

Roadrunners eat many kinds of food. They hunt insects and spiders. They catch scorpions too. They also eat lizards and small snakes. They catch mice.

These birds eat fruit and seeds. They find cactus fruit in the desert. This gives them water. It gives them energy too.

Roadrunners swallow small **prey** whole. Big meals are harder to eat. They bash big prey on rocks first. Then they can eat the smaller bites.

Roadrunners can eat small venomous rattlesnakes whole!

SPEEDY STRIKES
FUN FACT!
Roadrunners can snatch hummingbirds and other small birds right out of the air with a quick jump.

Pounce! A roadrunner leaps away from a striking snake. Eating can be dangerous!

Roadrunners are skilled hunters. They use speed and surprise to catch prey. A roadrunner can run 26 miles per hour while chasing food.

These birds grab prey with their strong beaks. They shake small animals back and forth. This stuns the prey quickly.

Roadrunners are brave hunters. They aren't afraid of rattlesnakes. They jump around the snake to confuse it. Then they strike at the snake's head.

Sometimes roadrunners hunt in pairs. One bird distracts the prey. The other attacks from behind.

WATCH OUT

Hiss! A snake slides by. The roadrunner must watch out.

Roadrunners have many enemies. Coyotes chase them on the ground. Hawks dive from the sky. Owls swoop down too.

Rattlesnakes can be a threat. Big roadrunners hunt snakes. But snakes also eat roadrunner eggs. They eat chicks too.

House cats raid nests. Raccoons do the same. They steal eggs when mom and dad leave. Roadrunners must stay alert to live.

Great horned owls hunt roadrunners at dawn and dusk. The low light helps them hunt.

RUN RUN
RUN

Whoosh! A roadrunner runs behind a bush. It is gone!

Roadrunners are good at getting away. They use their speed to zip between rocks and bushes.

These birds rarely fly to escape. Running is faster for them. They can turn very fast.

Their best defense is to hide in thick brush. Their streaky feathers help them blend in. Predators cannot see them. If they can't see them, they can't catch them!

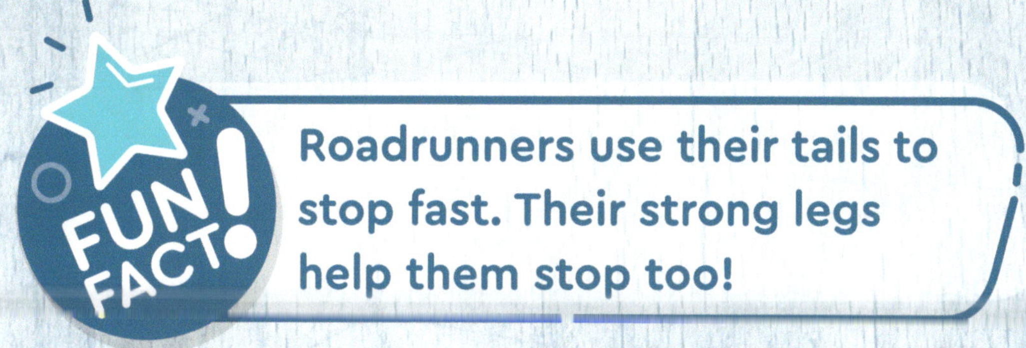

ZIPPY ZOOMERS

Thump! A roadrunner's feet pound the dirt. It zooms past a cactus.

Roadrunners are famous for their incredible speed. Their strong legs carry them across the desert floor faster than any other bird their size.

These birds take up to 12 steps per second. Each stride covers about 20 inches. That's 20 feet in one second!

Roadrunners use their long tails for balance. The tail helps them turn quickly at top speed.

Roadrunners can change direction mid-stride! Two toes point forward, two backward for grip.

DAY DASH

Chirp! The sun rises over the desert. A roadrunner starts its busy day.

Roadrunners wake up at dawn. They spend mornings hunting for food. This helps them avoid the midday heat.

By midday, the desert gets very hot. Roadrunners rest in the shade, finding cool spots under bushes or rocks.

In the late afternoon, they hunt again. They stay busy until sunset. Then they find a safe place to sleep.

Roadrunners sunbathe each morning! They spread their wings and fluff their back feathers to warm up.

SOLO STARS

Squawk! A roadrunner walks alone. It needs no flock.

Roadrunners live alone or in mating pairs. They do not form groups. Each bird hunts alone in its own area.

A roadrunner's territory can cover half a mile. The bird walks this space each day.

Some mated pairs stay together all year. The male and female guard their territory together. Other roadrunners like to live alone.

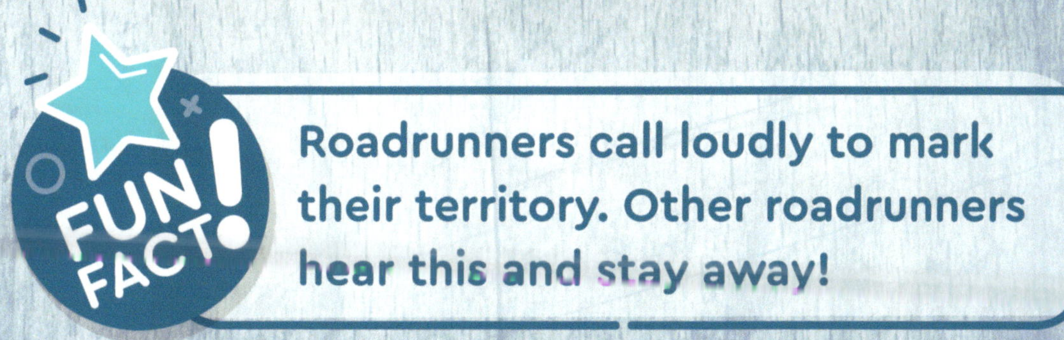

LOVE CALLS

Coo-coo! A male roadrunner bows low. He has a gift.

Male roadrunners bring food gifts to females. A male may offer a lizard or a snake. This shows he is a good hunter.

Males also make soft cooing sounds. They wag their tails up and down. Their head feathers stand up tall.

Once they mate, roadrunners can have two to six eggs. Both parents take turns sitting on the nest.

Roadrunner pairs stay together for life! They build nests and raise chicks as a team.

31

CUTE CHICKS
DID YOU KNOW?
Roadrunner parents sometimes feed their chicks scorpions! They remove the stinger first to keep babies safe.

Peep! Tiny chicks huddle in a nest. They wait for their parents to return.

Roadrunner chicks hatch after about 20 days. They are born with closed eyes and almost no feathers. Their skin looks pink and wrinkly.

Chicks grow fast. In just three weeks, they can leave the nest. They follow their parents to learn how to hunt.

Young roadrunners practice catching bugs and small lizards. By three weeks old, they can catch their own prey. Parents still help feed them, but most chicks leave home after about a month.

TEAM TEACH

Look! A roadrunner dad brings food. The hungry chicks chirp.

Both roadrunner parents work hard to raise their chicks. They take turns finding food. One parent guards the nest while the other hunts.

Parents also teach chicks how to catch prey. They show them how to grab bugs and lizards. Chicks watch and copy what they see.

Parents protect their chicks from weather too. At night, they keep chicks warm. During hot days, they shade the nest with their wings.

Parents may feed their hungry chicks every 15 to 20 minutes!

TOUGH
BIRDS

Crack! A roadrunner steps on a dry twig. It keeps walking.

Roadrunners are tough birds. They survive in extreme hot and cold. Deserts can be over 100 degrees. They can also drop below freezing at night.

On freezing cold nights, roadrunners slow their bodies way down. Their body temperature drops and they barely move at all. This saves energy so they do not need as much food to survive.

Roadrunners work in pairs to kill rattlesnakes. Two birds take turns. They peck the snake. The snake gets too tired to fight.

SPOT ONE

Look! A roadrunner hops onto a fence post. It scans the open land.

Want to spot a roadrunner? Look in open desert areas with low bushes. You can often find them along roadsides and trails.

Early morning is the best time to look. Roadrunners often sunbathe on rocks, spreading their wings to warm up.

Listen for their calls, too. A series of coos can lead you right to one.

Roadrunners are often seen running next to cars on desert roads! It's one of the easiest way to see one!

GLOSSARY

crest
A bunch of feathers that stick up on top of a bird's head.

adapted
Changed over time to live better in a certain place.

prey
An animal that is hunted and eaten by another animal.

venomous
Having poison that can hurt you with a bite or sting.

predators
Animals that hunt and eat other animals.